Curtain Up!

Behind the scenes at the
ROYAL OPERA HOUSE

ROYAL
OPERA
HOUSE

Ahh, there you are.
Welcome!
I'm Figaro, the resident cat here at the
Royal Opera House. I'm going to take you on
a secret backstage tour of this magnificent theater.
You'll meet a whole team of people working hard behind
the scenes to bring our ballets and operas to life.
You can also take a peek at the performers getting ready
for tonight's performance of *The Nutcracker* ballet.
We only have 30 minutes until the curtain rises
so there's no time for catnapping.
Follow me-ow!

Curtain Up!

Behind the scenes at the
ROYAL OPERA HOUSE

Illustrated by Lauren O'Hara

Contents

We'd better get going.
Follow me!

Costume Department

Your backstage tour begins here! It's the opening night of *The Nutcracker* and the costume department has been busy stitching and sewing 630 costumes for the performance. Some outfits are updated from the first time the production was put on, and some are made from scratch. Each costume has to be carefully fitted to the performer's body—if it is too tight, singing or dancing could be difficult. It looks like the tail on one of the mouse costumes has come loose. Luckily the costume team is on hand to make any last-minute repairs.

It takes 200 ft of stiff, net fabric to create a classical tutu like the Sugar Plum Fairy's in Act II of *The Nutcracker*. This tutu has 9 layers (plus a top skirt) but others can have up to 15. The layers are held together by swing catches—little threads that stop the tutu from separating and looking messy as the dancer moves around on stage.

With 30 minutes to curtain up, it's time for the dressers to make sure the costumes are ready to be moved to side stage. Sometimes a dancer can have as little as 45 seconds to change their costume, but luckily they will have one or two dressers to help them.

The other style of tutu is the Romantic tutu. This tutu is much longer and softer, and is worn by the snowflakes in *The Nutcracker*. A Romantic tutu is made up of around 75 ft of tulle, cut into 7 layers. The bottom layer is the stiffest, with finer and more supple layers on top. The Romantic tutu is designed to be light and float around the dancer's legs as they move.

Paw-don me. Coming through!

7

Wigs and Hats

Wig makers are hard at work in here, creating amazing hairstyles! A wig can transform a dancer or opera singer into their character. Look, there's the Sugar Plum Fairy's wig sprinkled with colorful glitter. It sparkles under the stage lights as she dances her *pas de deux*. The wig team creates more than 3,000 new wigs each year as well as looking after more than 100,000 wigs already in the collection. They also make hats, jewelry and tiaras to add the finishing touches to the performers' incredible outfits.

Six to eight weeks before a show starts, the wig team creates a mold of a performer's head so that their wig can be made the right size and shape. The wig sits on a rounded "wig block" to keep its shape while it is being styled and stored. Each wig takes over a week to make.

After a production is finished, wigs are carefully brushed, shampooed and conditioned before being reset with rollers. Rollers are used to help create waves in the hair and to shape it into different styles.

What are wigs made from?

Most styles of wig are made from human hair. Asian hair is used for very long styles. Natural blonde or white wigs are made from European hair. Wigs that have tall, complicated styles are not made from human hair, but yak hair.

The Queen of Hearts from *Alice's Adventures in Wonderland* has a bright red wig styled into a heart-shaped bun.

The Mad Hatter wears a bright green top hat and a shocking pink wig.

Carabosse, the wicked fairy in *The Sleeping Beauty*, has a wig of black curls and ringlets with a pair of sharp, pointed horns attached.

The White Rabbit's wig is shaped to look like a pair of rabbit ears.

10/6

The Queen of the Night from *The Magic Flute* wears an elaborate black wig and a wire crown. Her black veil is decorated with crystals which sparkle like stars in the night sky.

Costume jewelry is made from inexpensive metals, stones, sequins and wire. Clara, the heroine of *The Nutcracker*, wears a necklace made from imitation pearls.

I love purrrrls!

Pointe Shoe Room

Look at all these shoes! There can be no ballet performance without ballet slippers. After all, Cinderella wouldn't have found her way to the ball in bare feet! Slippers, boots, pointe and character shoes for the whole ballet company are stored in this room. A ballet company can get through up to 7,000 pairs a year! Satin pointe shoes come in pink and brown shades. Each pair has to be specially made to fit the dancer's feet. A **Principal** dancer can wear out a pair of pointe shoes in one performance.

What's the point of pointe shoes?

Pointe shoes make it possible for female ballet dancers to stand on the very tips of their toes. Professional dancers train for up to 10 years to be able to dance *en* **pointe**.

Male ballet dancers need to be able to make giant leaps and jumps in their shoes. They wear ballet slippers or special ballet boots made from soft leather or canvas. Male dancers sometimes wear pointe shoes to play comedy characters like Bottom in *The Dream*.

As soon as a dancer gets a new pair of pointe shoes, they start to break them in. New shoes are very hard and stiff so a dancer needs to soften the toe area, or "box," and crack the leather soles so that they are flexible enough for them to bend their feet. Dancers sew satin ribbons and elastics on to their shoes to keep them in place.

To make a pointe shoe, a shoemaker starts by wrapping layers of canvas and glue around the toe area of a foot-shaped mold to form the box. This will support the dancer's foot when they are up on their toes. The shoe is then hardened in an oven and covered in pink satin. A leather sole is attached to the bottom. Each shoemaker has a different way of making shoes and most dancers will use the same shoemaker for their whole career.

11

Scenery Department

It's time to swing by the scenery department, where the team has just finished decorating a 30 ft Christmas tree for tonight's performance. It is hung with over 100 twinkly candles and 200 shiny apples. Most of the large sets are created in a big warehouse before being transported to the Royal Opera House on a truck. It took 21 trucks to deliver all the sets and scenery for the Company's performance of Wagner's opera the *Ring* cycle!

Oops! I've got wet paint on my paws!

The **Theater Designer** starts by creating a small, 3D model of the set. This helps them to think about how they are going to build the set, what materials they are going to use and how the performers will move in the space (they make tiny model performers too!). The designer who created the town square set for the ballet *Don Quixote* even created mini model carts to work out how the dancers would wheel them on and off stage.

It's the **Production Assistant**'s job to draw up all the different parts of the theater designer's 3D model. The drawings are then passed on to the set builders who start constructing the set out of wood or metal.

All of the sets are painted carefully by hand. For the painted cloth background in *Swan Lake*, the **artist** started by painting a small version of the scene, 1/25th of the final size. They divided this image up into a grid and completed the final backdrop by painting one square at a time at a much bigger size.

Set Designers have to think about everything, from buildings and backgrounds to plants and trees. For the opera *Turandot*, the designer created a beautiful Chinese pagoda. For the ballet *The Winter's Tale,* the set team built a huge wishing tree with branches decorated with ribbons and jewels. This giant toadstool was made for the ballet *Alice's Adventures in Wonderland.*

Prop Department

There are all sorts of astonishing objects in here, from mysterious masks and musical instruments to huge, slithering serpents. Every item that appears on stage is made in the prop department using materials like papier-mâché, rubber and plastic. The props look very realistic, and they help to create mystery and surprise on stage. Tonight's performance includes a giant mechanical owl. As the bird flaps its wings, the character of Drosselmeyer magically appears from a secret door hidden behind it.

For the ballet *La Fille mal gardée,* which is set on a farm, the prop department had to make masks for the cast members that play the dancing chickens. In *The Nutcracker,* the army of mice is brought to life by skilled prop makers.

Sometimes dancers have to use props in their performance. The props need to be sturdy so that they don't fall apart on stage, but light enough to be easily carried. In *The Sleeping Beauty*, the **corps de ballet** perform a piece with garlands woven with fake flowers. In *Don Quixote*, the character Kitri dances a solo with a beautiful fan.

In the opera *The Magic Flute* one of the most important props is, of course, a flute. The prop department is often busy making instruments like tambourines for the Neapolitan dance in *Swan Lake*, or reed pipes for Act II of *The Nutcracker*.

If every so often the animals on stage look incredibly real, it's probably because they are! One production of the opera *Carmen* at the Royal Opera House starred a live horse and donkey. One ballet featured two white pigeons.

Puppets that dancers have to control on stage are some of the most complicated props to create. The giant Cheshire Cat in *Alice's Adventures in Wonderland* started out as a small paper model. Next the prop designers made a **maquette**— a full-size mock-up of the puppet. The dancers rehearsed with the maquette while the final cat was being built.

Armory

You'd better watch where you stand in this room—there are some sharp points! The armory department makes all the weapons used in performances. They create everything from imitation crossbows and swords to holsters and guns. They even make suits of armor! All the weapons are stored safely in a lockable box. Can you spot it over there? It contains the swords and rifles for *The Nutcracker's* toy soldiers and mice. The weapons are handed out to each performer before they step onto the stage. They have to bring them straight back afterwards.

Don't worry, I'm playing dead.

In tonight's performance there is a dramatic fight between the Mouse King and the Nutcracker. At the end of the fight, the dancer playing the defeated Mouse King has to "play dead" on stage. They lie perfectly still, only taking shallow breaths that the audience can't see. If a character has a gory end, they might squirt themselves with fake blood from the make-up department.

16

Learning the "Twyla"

Dancers learn a series of sword fighting movements to make sure no one gets injured on stage. The **"Twyla"** is made up of 8 positions in which the sword arm is moved left and right, and up and down. The dancers chant the pattern in their heads as they fight: up, up, down, up, down, down, up, down. They repeat the pattern in time with the music as they move across the stage. They need to concentrate—if anyone gets too caught up in the drama it could be dangerous!

In the ballet *Romeo and Juliet*, all the male dancers have to learn sword fighting skills because the metal swords they use need expert handling. Fight scenes look fast and furious to the audience, but they are carefully choreographed. The dancers learn each move and rehearse sword fighting routines alongside the dances in the ballet.

Ballet Studio

Take a quick peek inside this studio. There are only 20 minutes to go before curtain up and the stars of the show are making their final preparations for tonight's performance. Ballet dancers have to be incredibly fit to do their job. Every performer here has already done a full day of dancing. Even the most experienced dancers have a 90 minute ballet class in the morning to warm up their muscles. After that the Company rehearses 2 to 3 different ballets, with lunch, costume fittings and dress rehearsals in between!

plié

A ballet company is made up of different ranks of dancers. Newly joined dancers from ballet schools enter the **corps de ballet** of a company. They carry out group choreography within a ballet, such as the swans in *Swan Lake*. Advancing through the ranks, dancers take on solo parts through to leading roles. Different companies have varying ranks: for example, Artist, First Artist, Soloist, First Soloist, Principal and Principal Character Artist.

18

jeté

développé

arabesque

The **Stager** is responsible for teaching the dancers the choreography for a particular piece. They usually know the ballet very well and will have performed it themselves in the past.

The **Répétiteurs** are in charge of rehearsing the dancers for the ballet they will perform. During rehearsals, they make notes about the steps as the choreographer demonstrates them.

The **Choreographer** creates and arranges the dances in the ballet.

Costume Hall of Fame

Now head toward the dressing rooms, where you'll see a display of famous costumes from different operas and ballets. Some of the outfits are over 20 years old and are still worn in performances today! They are very delicate and have to be checked carefully after they are worn. The costumes for tonight's Sugar Plum Fairy and Prince are both embroidered with more than 500 tiny sequins and colorful stones.

Information about each outfit is kept in a costume bible. It includes the name of the costume designer, the original designs, the materials used and notes on how to make repairs. All the costumes are updated and refreshed each year to keep them looking as good as new. Did you know there's a whole room here just for dyeing fabrics?

If you look inside a costume, you will see a label with the name of the performance, the role and each performer who has worn it throughout history, carefully recorded.

Princess Turandot's costume from the opera *Turandot*. This outfit was designed in 1963 by the famous **costume designer** and **photographer** Cecil Beaton. Each piece, from the collar to the cloak, is decorated with appliqué. It would have been very heavy to wear.

Odette and Odile's tutus from the ballet *Swan Lake*. The roles of Odette, the swan-princess and Odile, the black swan, are danced by the same Principal ballerina.

Violetta's dress from the opera *La traviata*. Violetta's delicate white gown has been worn in performances of *La traviata* for 25 years. Costume designers have been very careful to repair it and make sure it is kept as close to the original dress as possible.

Costumes for the Firebird and Prince Ivan from *The Firebird* ballet. Prince Ivan's tunic is made from red and white taffeta and decorated with gold braid. The Firebird's elaborate tutu is made up of layers of yellow, orange and pink netting. The top layer has orange and yellow ribbons and feathers and flame-shaped tongues of red, orange and yellow satin edged with gold braid.

Rehearsal Room

Can you hear that? Even though tonight's performance is a ballet, right now, across the building, soloists, choruses and the Youth Opera Company are rehearsing for all sorts of musical performances. Singers rehearse together almost every day for at least a month before a show starts. It takes a lot of training and hard work to become an opera singer. Not only do they need to have perfect singing technique, a stage presence and great acting skills, but they also have to be fluent in lots of languages!

An opera singer needs to look after their vocal chords, just like an athlete looks after their body. They drink 70 to 100 oz of water a day to stay hydrated. If a singer feels their voice needs to recover, they spend some time on "vocal rest"—that means 48 hours of staying totally silent!

The people in this room are rehearsing the "Toreador Song" from *Carmen*. The song is sung by the character Escamillo who is accompanied by a group of singers called "the chorus." The role of Escamillo is performed by a bass-baritone.

Operas are performed in lots of different languages, like Italian, French, German, Russian and Czech. **Soloists** and the **chorus** rehearse with a **language coach** to make sure their pronunciation is perfect. Luckily the audience doesn't need to understand all these languages. During a performance there are **surtitles** in English above the stage.

In any single week the chorus often performs in 2 or 3 different productions. They will also be rehearsing 1 or 2 other productions during the day and learning the music for several other operas. That's a lot of music to remember!

Everyone can sing a different range of high and low notes. The 6 voice types from deepest to highest are: **bass**, **baritone**, **tenor**, **alto**, **mezzo-soprano** and **soprano**. In the opera *Hansel and Gretel*, the role of the boy Hansel is sung by a female mezzo-soprano and the evil Witch is sung by a male tenor.

Many people think that the most challenging opera to put on is Wagner's the *Ring* cycle. It is made up of 4 operas which take over 15 hours to perform! The characters include Wotan, King of the Gods, his daughter mighty warrior Brünnhilde and the dragon Fafner.

This soprano is preparing for her role as the Queen of the Night in *The Magic Flute*. She is rehearsing an **aria**. An aria is where the action of the story pauses while the character sings a solo piece to the audience.

Dressing Room

With just 15 minutes to go, the performers are in their dressing rooms adding final touches to their hair and make-up. Each performer has their own dressing space where they keep their make-up, hair pins and brushes and carefully lay out their costumes and ballet shoes. Performers decorate their spaces with photos and good-luck charms. The dressing rooms have speakers so that the performers can hear the orchestra warming up and the buzz as the audience begin to take their seats in the auditorium. Any minute now they'll hear an announcement telling them that it's time to make their way to the stage.

Every dressing table has a mirror with special lighting that imitates the bright lighting on stage. The audience cannot see the performers' faces clearly from a distance, so stage make-up exaggerates their features and expressions.

24

If a performer needs to wear prosthetic make-up like a fake nose or a gruesome wound, now is the time to make sure it's properly fixed in place. Male ballet dancers performing roles like Kostcheï in *The Firebird* or the Duchess in *Alice's Adventures in Wonderland* need to leave plenty of time to prepare, because they wear fake noses and lots of make-up.

Each dancer has their own basket which they take to side stage before the performance. In it they keep everything they might need, from blister Band-Aids to scissors and even bottles of nail polish to make emergency repairs to runs in their tights.

25

Orchestra Pit

Shhhh! The musicians have fallen silent, ready to begin. They sit in the orchestra pit, tucked just below the stage. The pit has special walls to create the perfect acoustics—sound that is loud enough for the audience to hear without being too loud for the performers on stage. The music for tonight's ballet was composed by Pyotr Il'yich Tchaikovsky. Tchaikovsky also composed the music for *Swan Lake* and *The Sleeping Beauty*. Can you spot the conductor? She's the last person to arrive before the performance starts. It's show time!

The **conductor** makes sure that everyone keeps to the same tempo. They stand on a small platform so that the whole orchestra can see them. The **musicians** are arranged into four groups and the conductor uses their arms (or sometimes a baton) to direct them, telling each group when to start and stop, when to play softly and when to get louder.

Brass instruments are the loudest, so they sit at the back. Brass instruments in an orchestra usually include the trumpet, French horn, trombone and the tuba.

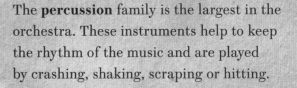

The **percussion** family is the largest in the orchestra. These instruments help to keep the rhythm of the music and are played by crashing, shaking, scraping or hitting.

Woodwind instruments sit in the middle of the orchestra. These instruments are played by blowing air through a mouthpiece and opening and closing holes in the instrument with the musician's fingers. The highest sound is made by a small flute called the piccolo and the lowest sound is made by the bassoon.

Stringed instruments produce a soft sound, and they are positioned at the front of the orchestra so they can be heard. High-pitched strings, like violins, violas and sometimes harps, sit on the conductor's left. The lower-pitched cellos and double basses sit on the right.

On the stage tonight

The production of *The Nutcracker* onstage tonight was created by choreographer Sir Peter Wright. It was first performed at the Royal Opera House in 1984 and has been one of The Royal Ballet's most popular productions ever since. It is based on the original ballet of *The Nutcracker* which was first performed in St Petersburg, Russia, in 1892. The ballet was inspired by E.T.A Hoffmann's Christmas fairytale about a young girl's magical adventure.

The story of the ballet – Act 1

The curtain rises on a Christmas Eve party at the home of Mayor Stahlbaum, his wife and their children, Clara and Fritz. Clara is given a nutcracker toy by her godfather, Drosselmeyer. Clara creeps downstairs to take a last look at the toy before bed. As midnight strikes, magical things begin to happen.

The whole room is growing—even the Christmas tree! Clara's nutcracker doll comes to life. Giant mice appear and the now man-sized Nutcracker leads an army of toy soldiers into battle. Clara helps the Nutcracker defeat the Mouse King. Clara rushes to the Nutcracker, injured from battle. But before her eyes he turns into a handsome prince called Hans-Peter!

Act 2

Clara and the Nutcracker Prince journey to the Kingdom of Sweets where Drosselmeyer hosts a celebration of their bravery. They are entertained with a wonderful display of dances from around the world. Finally the Sugar Plum Fairy and her **cavalier** perform a dance before waving Clara and the Nutcracker Prince off on their sleigh. The next morning, Clara wakes up back at home, but her adventures seem to have been more than just a dream.

Meet the characters

Clara (right) is the eldest child of Mr and Mrs Stahlbaum. She is given a shiny wooden Nutcracker doll by her godfather, Drosselmeyer, on Christmas Eve. Once nighttime falls, she finds herself in the middle of a wonderful adventure!

The **Sugar Plum Fairy** (below) is the ruler of the Kingdom of Sweets. She welcomes Clara and Hans-Peter to her kingdom.

Drosselmeyer (above) is Clara's godfather. He entrusts Clara with the Nutcracker doll, which is very special to him. He is Hans-Peter's uncle.

Hans-Peter (left) is the nephew of Drosselmeyer. He was turned into a wooden Nutcracker doll by the evil Mouse King's mother. His uncle Drosselmeyer has been searching for someone to help break the spell.

The **Mouse King** (right) leads an army of mice. When he is defeated, the spell on the Nutcracker is broken and Hans-Peter is turned back into a young man.

Side Stage

Quick, there's no time to rest, there's a whole team of performers, crew, technicians and managers positioned backstage ready to deliver the perfect performance. They all have to work together to make sure it goes without a hitch. You will get to see the complicated operations that take place out of sight of the audience. The stage here has a special wagon system of movable floors that allow scene changes during a performance. There are 21 wagons for opera productions and 6 with specially sprung floors for ballet productions. Can you imagine coordinating all that?

It's a **Stage Manager**'s job to make sure that everything runs smoothly on the night. They check that the stage and all the special effects are safe for the performers and they deal with any problems that occur during the performance.

The **hydraulics operator** controls the parts of the set and stage that move up and down. When the character of Drosselmeyer appears to float on stage, he's actually standing on a secret platform controlled by the hydraulics operator.

The **Assistant Stage Managers** work in the wings, making sure the props are ready and the singers or dancers enter the stage at the right time.

The **Flys department** is in charge of the special effects. For *The Nutcracker*, they control the snow shaker from high up in the fly tower, looking down as the fake snowflakes flutter onto the dancers below.

Some performances have flame effects, explosions or smoke. These are carefully controlled by the **pyrotechnics team**, who tests the effects before the performance or during the intermission. A **firefighter** stands by in case of an emergency.

The **Deputy Stage Manager** has an important job to do during a live performance. They follow the music and give cues to all the departments so that everything happens at exactly the right moment.

33

Encore! How can I get involved?

The performance is over, but don't worry, it doesn't have to end here. There are plenty of ways that you can get involved in ballet or opera. Perhaps you want to be a dancer or a singer? Or maybe you would like to be a conductor, a set designer or a stage manager? Whatever it is you want to do, you can start learning the skills.

Why not try taking a ballet or dance class? If you are really serious about becoming a member of a ballet company it is going to take a lot of training and hard work.

If you would like to be in an orchestra you'll need to learn an instrument. First, think carefully about what you'd like to play. Why not ask your school if you can try one or two instruments before you decide? Then practice, practice, practice!

If you have a big imagination and love being creative, then working in the costume department could be the job for you. Why not make an outfit for your favorite character from old clothes or material you have at home?

Becoming a member of a junior choir is a great way to start singing and learn to read music. If you don't have a choir near you, ask your school if you can start one with some friends.

Joining an art club will teach you lots of skills that you could use as a prop or set designer. There are also plenty of projects that you could try at home. How about building your own set from cardboard boxes? Or try your hand at making some fake food from papier-mâché!

Glossary

Acoustics
The features of a room or space which make sound easy or difficult to hear.

Act
A portion of an opera or ballet. Most ballets and operas have three acts.

Alto
A low female singing voice.

Appliqué
A sewing technique where smaller pieces of fabric are stitched onto a large piece of fabric creating a pattern or design. The pieces of fabric are usually covered in decorative stitching.

Arabesque
The arabesque is a position in ballet where the dancer balances on one leg and extends the other leg out behind the body. Both legs are straight. The arms are held out elegantly.

Arias
A solo piece in an opera sung by a main character, in which they show their thoughts or emotions.

Audience
A group that listens to or watches a concert, performance or play.

Auditorium
A part of a theater where the audience sits.

Baritone
The middle male singing voice, between bass and tenor.

Bass
The lowest male singing voice.

Baton
A thin stick used by a conductor to direct an orchestra or choir.

Canvas
A strong and rough type of woven material.

Cavalier
The male dancer who is the partner of
a ballerina.

Choreographer
The person who creates and arranges
the dances in a ballet.

Choreography
The art of creating and arranging dances for
a performance, especially dance and ballet.

Chorus
A group of people who sing together.

Composer
A person who writes music.

Corps de ballet
The dancers in a ballet company who perform
as a group and don't have any solo parts.

Cue
A signal for a performer to enter the stage or begin
their performance, or, for a crew member to get ready
to carry out one of their tasks during the performance.

Développé
The smooth, gradual unfolding of the leg. The dancer
raises the thigh to the side with the knee bent, then
straightens the leg to the front, side, or back.

Jeté
A leap or jump where a dancer takes off from one foot and lands on the other. The leaping leg is extended to the front or side while in the air.

Maquette
A small scale model or rough draft of a sculpture or puppet.

Mezzo-soprano
The middle female singing voice, between alto and soprano.

Papier-mâché
A light, strong material made of pieces of paper mixed with glue.

Pas de deux
A dance for two people, usually a man and a woman.

Plié
Bending the knees with hips, legs and feet turned out.

Embroidery
The art of decorating material or fabric with patterns created with a needle and thread.

Fly tower
A system for moving sets and equipment. The fly tower at the Royal Opera House is 120 ft high.

Intermission
A break between parts of a performance when the audience can leave their seats.

Pointe
A ballet position where the dancer balances
on the toes of their shoes.

Prosthetics
A type of make-up where flexible material is applied
to a person's face or body to change their appearance.

Satin
A smooth, glossy material.

Soprano
The highest female singing voice.

Surtitles
Captions displayed alongside an opera that translate
the language it is being performed in into English.

Taffeta
A shiny, stiff material.

Tempo
The speed at which a piece of music
should be played.

Tenor
The highest male singing voice.

Tulle
A fine, lightweight netting that
is used a lot in ballet costumes.

Tutu
The layered skirt worn by
a female ballet dancer.
A classical tutu is short and
stiff to show the dancer's legs.
A Romantic tutu is softer
and falls to below the calf.

Wagon
A large, wheeled platform
or floor which can be moved
around the stage by the crew.
The wagon system at the
Royal Opera House allows
the crew to change scenes
in as little as 40 seconds.